Drag

RACING

By Alex Monnig

SportsZone

An Imprint of Abdo Publishing
www.abdopublishing.com

www.abdopublishing.com

Published by Abdo Publishing, a division of ABDO, PO Box 398166, Minneapolis, Minnesota 55439. Copyright © 2015 by Abdo Consulting Group, Inc. International copyrights reserved in all countries. No part of this book may be reproduced in any form without written permission from the publisher. SportsZone™ is a trademark and logo of Abdo Publishing.

Printed in the United States of America, North Mankato, Minnesota
042014
092014

THIS BOOK CONTAINS
RECYCLED MATERIALS

Cover Photo: NHRA, Jerry Foss/AP Images
Interior Photos: NHRA, Jerry Foss/AP Images, 1; Gainesville Sun, Brad McClenny/AP Images, 4–5; RacersEdgePhotography, Ken Sklute/AP Images, 6; AP Images, 8, 12–13, 22, 41; Derek Yegan/Shutterstock Images, 10; Stephen Griffith/Shutterstock Images, 15; SIM via Getty Images, 16; Juerg Schreiter/Shutterstock Images, 18; Action Sports Photography/Shutterstock Images, 20–21, 25, 33; Phillip Rubino/Shutterstock Images, 26, 28–29, 36; Steve Mann/Shutterstock Images, 30–31; NHRA, Marc Gewertz/AP Images, 34; Seth Rossman/AP Images, 38–39; NHRA, Teresa Long/AP Images, 43; Mindy Schauer, Orange County Register/AP Images, 44

Editor: Patrick Donnelly
Series Designer: Craig Hinton

Library of Congress Control Number: 2014932864

Cataloging-in-Publication Data
Monnig, Alex.
 Drag racing / Alex Monnig.
   p. cm. -- (Inside the speedway)
Includes bibliographical references and index.
ISBN 978-1-62403-402-2
1. Drag racing--Juvenile literature. I. Title.
796.72--dc23

2014932864

TABLE OF CONTENTS

1 The Run.....................................5

2 California Cruising.....................13

3 Dynamite Dragsters.....................21

4 Ready to Race............................31

5 Legendary Drag Racers...............39

Glossary 46

For More Information 47

Index 48

About the Author 48

chapter 1

THE RUN

Drag racer Tony Schumacher was no stranger to winning. He had already won the top fuel division of the National Hot Rod Association (NHRA) Drag Racing Series in 1999, 2004, and 2005. However, his odds of winning a fourth title in 2006 looked slim.

He started the season poorly. But he soon began charging toward the top of the season standings. Schumacher reached second place on the leaderboard by the final race of the season. It was the Auto Club Finals.

Tony Schumacher is one of the most successful drag racers of all time.

Doug Kalitta was edged out by Tony Schumacher for the 2006 NHRA Top Fuel championship.

He would have to win two more rounds (also called passes) than leader Doug Kalitta won that night. Schumacher also needed to break a national speed record. That would give him 20 bonus points in the standings and put him in first place.

Both men won their first two races. But then Schumacher's luck improved. Melanie Troxel beat Kalitta in the third round. Meanwhile, Schumacher won his third-round pass. He headed to the final against Troxel.

The entire season came down to one single race. The title would be decided in the blink of an eye. The title would be Schumacher's if he won and finished the pass in less than 4.437 seconds to set the record.

The cars did their usual burnouts at the start of the race and made their way to the starting line. The light turned from amber to green. Both drivers gunned their engines. Then Schumacher sped ahead and left Troxel in the dust. He had won. But was his time good enough? The clock at the end of the track flashed 4.428 seconds. Schumacher had traveled

Terrific Tony

Tony Schumacher was not done winning championships in 2006. In 2009 he became the first driver to win six consecutive NHRA Top Fuel season titles. That gave him seven overall. As of 2013, the man nicknamed "The Sarge" races for his father Don Schumacher's racing team.

Funny car driver Scott Kalitta was killed in a fiery crash in 2008. His death led drag racing officials to shorten the distance of funny car and top fuel races.

at 327.98 miles per hour (mph) to beat the odds. That is approximately 528 kilometers per hour (km/h). His victory became known simply as "The Run." It is widely considered the greatest finish to an NHRA season.

Schumacher's 2006 victory showcased the thrills and drama drag racing can provide. Each race features two vehicles, usually cars, lined up side-by-side. They race each other in a straight line to the finish. The cars cover the 1,000-foot (305-meter) track in amazing times of less than five seconds. The vehicles can reach speeds as fast as 330 mph (531 km/h).

There are different drag racing series all over the world. The one that started it all is the NHRA Drag Racing Series in the United States. Drivers compete in 24 races throughout the season. The drivers earn points based on how they finish at each event. They also receive bonus points in the season standings for setting speed records.

Each of the 24 events is broken into different divisions that feature different vehicles. The major four divisions are top fuel, funny car, pro stock cars, and pro stock motorcycle. Drivers are sponsored by teams. The teams provide the vehicles and a crew.

Track Change

Drag racing tracks were usually one-quarter mile (0.4 km) long until 2008. That was when driver Scott Kalitta died in a tragic accident. Scott was Doug Kalitta's cousin. To make the races less dangerous, the NHRA shortened the track for funny car and top fuel races to 1,000 feet (305 m).

The crew works on the vehicles on and off the track. There are rules and regulations for this dangerous and exciting sport now. But that was not the case when the first drag racers started battling each other in California decades ago.

chapter 2

CALIFORNIA CRUISING

Drag racing has come a long way. At first it was an illegal activity. Then one man helped turn it into a sport. Now drag racing has organized competitions and rules. Some races are even shown on TV.

An early form of drag racing started in the 1930s in California. Owners wanted to test their cars against other people's cars. But they did not want to worry about obstacles and turns. All the drivers cared about was

A starter leaps in the air and waves a flag to start a drag race in 1954.

Dragsters used to race each other on city streets. Now races are held at tracks specifically designed for drag racing.

showing off speed. So they decided to race in dry lake beds. That setting allowed them to drive in a straight line without turning. The standard road length for the races was one-quarter mile (0.4 km).

Cars started to get faster and faster. Soon drivers were reaching 100 mph (161 km/h). It was a dangerous hobby. There were no barriers to separate the spectators from the speeding cars. And the drivers did not have safety gear.

But the drivers still wanted to go faster. They started spending more time tinkering with their cars. They wanted to prove who was the fastest. Sometime in the 1940s, racing moved to the streets. It also started to become more popular. Books and movies

Deciding on Drag Racing

The name *drag racing* has unclear origins. Some think it started with people dragging their cars out to race. Others say it has to do with streets in towns being called "the main drag." There is also a driving method called dragging that involves keeping the car in gear longer. That could have something to do with the name too.

In the 1950s drag racing moved from the streets to drag strips like this one in Kansas City, Missouri.

came out about drag racing. They made the dangerous activity seem cool to a young audience.

Wally Parks spent his teenage years in California. He fell in love with drag racing. Parks remained interested in the sport as he grew older. In 1947 he helped organize the Southern California Timing Association (SCTA). Two years later the SCTA held its first "Speed Week." At the event, drivers raced against the clock instead of each other.

The Santa Ana Drags opened in Southern California in 1950. It was the first official drag strip. It was built on an airstrip. Fans could sit in the grandstands while watching. Many were fascinated by the track's computerized speed clocks. The clocks led to more accurate timing for the super-fast machines.

The sport took a giant leap forward in 1951. That is when Parks formed the NHRA. It helped create specific rules for drag racing. The NHRA set standards that cars had to meet in order to race. More important, the NHRA also set up safety rules. Now races could take place at tracks all around the country using the same regulations.

The first NHRA race with the standard rules was held in April 1953 in California. Two years later the organization took its show on the road. The 1955 NHRA Nationals took place in Kansas. That was when the sport began hopping around the

A set of lights known as a "Christmas tree" tells drag racers when they can take off.

country. More and more fans had the chance to watch the races in person.

Improvements in technology led to better competition and faster machines. Race starts were also redesigned with a new format. Originally a person stood between the two cars. That person waved a flag when it was time for the cars to take off. That changed in 1963. An electronic light system called a "Christmas tree" was introduced. A series of lights of different colors told racers when it was time to take off.

In 1974 the NHRA began awarding points based on where racers finished. That year it also named its first national series champions. More races were added as years passed. At the same time, racers reached more speed records. And, most important, more rules were added to keep drivers safe.

chapter 3

DYNAMITE DRAGSTERS

Drag racing vehicles have improved over time. At first teenagers just made changes to their everyday cars. Then they drove those "souped-up" vehicles in races. Eventually people started building vehicles designed just to speed down quarter-mile tracks. There are now four main classifications of cars used in drag racing. They are top fuel, funny car, pro stock car, and pro stock motorcycle.

Top fuel machines are among the fastest racing vehicles in the world.

Don "Big Daddy" Garlits, shown winning a race in 1968, helped invent a car with the engine behind the driver after he lost part of his right foot in a crash.

Top fuel machines are the fastest drag racing vehicles. They are longer and skinnier than normal cars. They are usually about 25 feet (7.6 m) long. Their back wheels are larger than the front ones. Top fuel cars can reach maximum speeds of

100 mph (161 km/h) in less than one second. They have been timed going more than 330 mph (531 km/h).

Drivers sit toward the back of the car with the long, skinny part in front of them. The engines are behind the drivers and between the bigger wheels. But that was not always the case. The engines used to sit in front of the drivers. That changed after popular driver Don "Big Daddy" Garlits had a major accident in 1970. Garlits was experimenting with a two-speed transmission. But early in the race, his engine exploded. In the wreck, his car was ripped into two pieces. But the car was not the only casualty of the explosion. Garlits also lost part of his right foot in the wreck.

But Big Daddy would not be defeated. Instead, Garlits went to work fixing the problem. He was tired of being in danger sitting behind the hot, heavy engines. He thought it made more sense to put the most dangerous components of the car behind the driver. So he helped invent a car with the engine in the back. Critics thought his new design would not be as fast as the old dragsters. It did not take Garlits long to prove them wrong. The very next year, he took his car, "Swamp Rat XIV," to the finals of its first race. He soon became the first driver to win an NHRA national event in a rear-engine dragster. By 1972 all cars had engines in the back instead of the front.

Funny cars have a silly name, but their power is no joke. They are almost as fast as top fuel cars. Funny cars are also shorter than top fuel cars. But they can still race down the track at about 315 mph (507 km/h). Funny cars look more like standard race cars. But drivers lift the entire top shell of the body off the frame to take their seat. The body is made of a lightweight carbon alloy that increases speed.

Pro stock cars look similar to everyday cars on the outside. The major differences are hidden

Safety First

More speed means more danger. In 1959 the NHRA made a rule that drag racers going over 150 mph (241 km/h) had to have a parachute braking system. Now a parachute flies out from the back of those cars when they brake at the end of a race. And a 1971 rule required all cars to carry a fire extinguisher.

Drag racers rely on a parachute brake system to help slow the cars after they cross the finish line.

inside. Pro stock engines are supercharged versions of normal

ones. Because of that extra power, the frame of the car has to

be extra durable. The chassis and the suspension are stronger

to handle the sudden acceleration of the vehicle.

Pro stock motorcycles are much larger than the motorcycles people drive on the street.

Pro stock motorcycles, on the other hand, look quite different from everyday models. The bodies of racing bikes are much larger. The areas behind the front wheel and behind the driver's seat are filled out more. Another notable difference is an extra piece connected to the back of the bike. It looks like training wheels from a child's bicycle. These tiny wheels help keep the bike in control at speeds of up to 195 mph (314 km/h). Control is especially important at the start. The sudden acceleration can make the front tire of the bike pop off the ground into a wheelie.

All types of drag racing vehicles use special tires. They are made to deal with the incredible power and heat created by the cars. The tires also have special treads that provide more traction. That helps them grip the track at high speeds.

DRAG Photo Diagram

1. **BACK TIRES:** The large tires help keep the car on the ground and moving in a straight line when drivers gun it at the start of races.

2. **DRIVER'S SEAT:** The place where the driver operates the vehicle is toward the back of the car, but in front of the engine.

3. **BODY:** This is made of lightweight material, usually carbon composite, for maximum speed.

4. **ROLL CAGE:** Bars that surround the driver's head for protection in a crash.

5. **REAR WING:** Like the large back tires, it also helps handle the extreme power and pressure at the start of the race to keep the car on the ground.

6. **EXHAUST:** The excess energy from the engine reaction goes here when the car is in motion. Often flames will shoot out from the car because so much power is being used.

READY TO RACE

Drag racing is more complicated than it might appear at first glance. Many things can go wrong before and during a race. Drivers need to keep their cool as they fly down the track at top speeds in extreme heat created by the big engines and skidding tires.

Some of the most important skills in drag racing are applied before the car even hits the track. How a car is put together is just as

Drag racers and their crews work long hours getting their vehicles ready for races.

Drag racers in the same class might look very similar, but no two vehicles are exactly alike.

important as how it is driven. Crew members work long hours to get everything perfect before race day.

Small details become big deals in drag racing. Teams have to find the right balance for the weight of the vehicle. If a car is too heavy it will be too slow. If it is too light it will not be able to withstand the pressure and power needed to race.

No two drag racing vehicles are exactly the same. They all have the same general parts, including engines, chassis, and tires. But the weight and feel of each dragster is different. Riders spend hours in their cars before they are comfortable and have total

Don "Snake" Prudhomme

Don Prudhomme is considered one of the best drag racers of all time. One reason he earned that reputation is because he had such good starts. He earned the nickname "Snake" because of his quick-striking reflexes at the beginning of races. From 1975 to 1976, Prudhomme won 13 of the 16 national NHRA events. He retired in 1994 with 35 funny car victories and 14 top fuel wins. That gave him more victories than any nitro fuel racer in NHRA history at the time.

control of them. That means they must practice the short races over and over again.

Body control is also important. This is especially true for pro stock motorcyclists. Their bikes are built so the riders can lean far forward. It almost looks like they are lying down on their stomachs. This allows them to be more aerodynamic. That means the wind does not slow them down as much.

Drag racers need to have good timing too. Even the smallest mistake can make the difference between winning and losing. One of the worst mistakes a driver can make on race day is not being ready at the starting line. Drivers need to have good reaction time. That means they have to be able to step on the gas as soon as the signal in front of them turns green. Drivers can do exercises to improve reaction time.

But the importance of timing does not end at the starting line. Drivers need to shift gears while driving to go the fastest.

Drag racers do "burnouts" at the starting line to heat up their tires as they wait for the green light.

Shifting to higher gears allows a car to go faster. Smooth gear changes help the car efficiently reach maximum speed. Sloppy shifting can lead to defeat.

Drag races are over in about five seconds. That seems like a small amount of time, and it is. But a lot can go wrong in that short time span. Traveling at such high speeds over such short distances is different than cruising down the highway. At any moment the car can spin and flip out of control. Racers have to be prepared to handle any situation that might arise during a race.

chapter 5

LEGENDARY DRAG RACERS

Cars are much faster now than they were in 1951 when the NHRA was created. Speed records have continued to fall. One man was responsible for breaking a lot of them in the early years of organized drag racing. He was the same man who helped make dragsters what they are today.

Don "Big Daddy" Garlits was one of the first superstars of drag racing. In 1964 Garlits became the first driver to reach

Don "Big Daddy" Garlits won 17 national championships and was the biggest name in drag racing for decades.

200 mph (322 km/h) in a race. In 1975 he was the first driver to top 250 mph (402 km/h). Garlits started his career in Florida. That is on the other side of the United States from California, where drag racing first took off. But before long, he was known to race fans around the country.

In 2001 Garlits was named the top drag racer of the first 50 years of the NHRA. One look at his career makes it easy to see why. He captured 17 national championships from 1958 to 1992. Garlits was also responsible for one of the most important changes in drag racing history. He led the charge to put engines behind drivers instead of in front of them.

Driver Shirley Muldowney was the best female drag racer of all time. She shared some of the spotlight with her friend Garlits. Simply competing on the NHRA circuit is hard. But women had

He Said It

"I liked the idea of two cars lined up side by side, not bumping into one another. It was one person against one person, one machine against one machine. There was a winner and a loser. It was real simple."
—*Don Garlits on why he enjoyed drag racing*

Shirley Muldowney proved to the world that women could compete with men in drag racing.

to overcome additional challenges. Some drivers and fans thought the track was no place for women.

Muldowney proved them wrong. She started her career as a successful funny car racer. But crashes and dangerous fires made her switch to top fuel. There she really shined. Muldowney was the first driver, male or female, to win three top fuel championships. She did so in 1977, 1980, and 1982.

In 1984 she was in a horrible crash at an event in Quebec, Canada. Some people thought she would never race again. But Muldowney was behind the wheel again in 1987. Two years later she won her eighteenth NHRA event. It was her last victory. She retired in 2003.

John Force is one of the biggest stars in the modern era of drag racing. Force became the face of drag racing for a new era of fans. It helps when you have spent as much time in the winner's circle as Force has.

Force won his first race in 1987. Then the wins kept coming. From 1993 to 2002 he won a record 10 funny car championships in a row. In 1996 he became the first drag racer to be named Driver of the Year by the National Motorsports Press Association. He won his sixteenth funny car championship in 2013 at age 64. That made him the oldest world champion in NHRA history.

John Force's daughters—from left, Courtney, Brittany, and Ashley—followed in their father's footsteps to become successful drag racers.

But Force has become more than just a driver. He is the head of a drag racing empire. John Force Racing is one of the most popular teams in the sport. And John is not the only Force tearing it up on the track. His daughter Brittany is a top fuel driver. Another of his daughters, Courtney, competes in funny cars, while daughter Ashley raced funny cars until she started her own family. And his son-in-law, Robert Hight, is the president of John Force Racing and also drives funny cars.

Force is one of the most powerful and successful people in drag racing. But drivers such as Garlits and Muldowney helped pave the way for him and his daughters. Only time will tell who will take down the next speed barrier in the exciting sport of drag racing.

GLOSSARY

ACCELERATION
When a car increases speed.

AERODYNAMICS
How air flowing around a car can affect its speed and handling.

BURNOUT
When a driver spins the tires quickly in place to heat them up and clean them.

CHASSIS
The frame of a car.

CLASSIFICATIONS
Grouping similar vehicles to separate the different types of drag racing.

CREW
A group of people working on the cars and helping drivers race.

DURABLE
Strong or able to withstand stress.

SERIES
A set of races in which riders compete throughout a season.

STOCK CAR
A standard car that is modified for racing.

TRACTION
The grip that allows a tire to stay on the ground.

FOR MORE INFORMATION

Further Readings

Arneson, Erik. *John Force: The Straight Story of Drag Racing's 300-mph Superstar*. Osceola, WI: Motorbooks, 2009.

Keenan, Patrick J. *The Ultimate Guide to NHRA Drag Racing Statistics*. Frederick, MD: Publish America, 2012.

Miller, Timothy. *Drag Racing: The World's Fastest Sport*. Buffalo, NY: Firefly Books, 2012.

Muldowney, Shirley. *Tales From a Top Fuel Dragster: A Collection of the Greatest Drag Racing Stories Ever Told*. New York: Sports Publishing, 2013.

Reyes, Steve. *The Dawn of Pro Stock: Drag Racing's Fastest Doorslammers: 1970–1979*. NorthBranch, MN: CarTech, 2012.

Websites

To learn more about Inside the Speedway, visit **booklinks.abdopublishing.com**. These links are routinely monitored and updated to provide the most current information available.

INDEX

Auto Club Finals, 5

engines, 23–24, 25, 32

Force, Ashley, 44–45
Force, Brittany, 44
Force, Courtney, 44
Force, John, 42, 44–45
funny car, 9, 21, 24, 32, 41, 42, 44–45

Garlits, Don, 23–24, 39–40, 45

Hight, Robert, 45

Kalitta, Doug, 6–7
Kalitta, Scott, 9

Muldowney, Shirley, 40–42, 45

NHRA, 5, 7, 8, 9, 17, 19, 24, 32, 39, 40, 42
NHRA Nationals, 17

Parks, Wally, 16, 17
pro stock car, 9, 21, 24
pro stock motorcycle, 9, 21, 26–27
Prudhomme, Don, 32

safety measures, 9, 14, 17, 19, 24
Santa Ana Drags, 17
Schumacher, Don, 7
Schumacher, Tony, 5–8
SCTA, 16–17
Speed Week, 17

tires, 27
top fuel, 5–8, 9, 21, 22–24, 32, 41, 44
Troxel, Melanie, 7

About the Author

Alex Monnig is a freelance journalist from St. Louis, Missouri. He graduated with his master's degree from the University of Missouri in May 2010. During his career, he has spent time covering sporting events around the world, including the 2008 Olympic Games in China, the 2011 Rugby World Cup in New Zealand, and the 2014 Olympic Games in Sochi, Russia.